WORLD
WITHOUT
END

WORLD
WITHOUT
END

Dan Masterson

THE UNIVERSITY OF ARKANSAS PRESS

FAYETTEVILLE   1991   LONDON

95 94 93 92 91   5 4 3 2 1

This book was designed by Ch. H. Russell
using the Janson typeface.

The paper used in this publication meets the minimum require-
ments of the American National Standard for Permanence of
Paper for Printed Library Materials Z39.48-1984. ⊚

Library of Congress Cataloging-in-Publication Data

Masterson, Dan, 1934-
        World without end / Dan Masterson.
            p.   cm.
        ISBN 1-55728-177-7 (alk. paper) .
        ISBN 1-55728-178-5 (pbk. : alk. paper)
        I. Title
        PS3563. A834W67   1991
        811' .54--dc20   90-10890
                                                        CIP

for Janet, whose reverence
for the natural world
is Senecan, her presence
within it, serene

ACKNOWLEDGMENTS

The author is grateful to the editors of the publications in which the following poems first appeared:

"Connemara," *Southern Review*; "Starting Over," "Snack," "The List," *Prairie Schooner*; "Fresh-Kill Report," *New York Quarterly*; "Bat," *The Ontario Review*; "Purple Finch," "Locked in the Icehouse," "Aunt Sadie's Carrot Juice," *Poetry Northwest*; "Heron," *Ploughshares*; "Getting Ready for Snow," *The North American Review*; "Leaving," *The Back Door*; "After Three Days Alone," *Bergen Poets*; "Bloodline," *Poetry Miscellany*; "Redtail," *Redme*; "Cabin Fever," *Caprice*; "White-Tail," *North Dakota Quarterly*; "Varying Hare," "Beaver," "Mink," "Chow Chow," *North Atlantic Quarterly*; "Particulars," *Crazyhorse*; "Warning to Tourists," "Note to Summer Renters," *Wordsmith*; "Coulter's Road," "She Wanted to Know," *The South Carolina Review*; "Rudy," *The Gettysburg Review*.

Contents

WORLD
WITHOUT
END

Heron

Late August, and the pond is holding
the summer's heat close to shore
where leaf-litter has begun to form;
even out at the center of things
there are pockets of warmth
deep beneath a canoe short-roped
to a slab of scrap iron heaved into place
once again on a scrub-topped boulder
barely covered by water.

The swimmer is up from his dive,
settling flatout aside the makeshift anchor,
far from the potbelly smoke
drifting from his empty cabin losing
itself in the high peaks
of the Adirondacks, the noon sun
drying him out full length.

He stands, then hunkers down
on the rock, rubbing himself hard
with open hands, his hair running
what feels like snowmelt down
across his shoulders as he searches

the vacant sky, the disturbed water
coming from the inlet.

It is another ending, the last
swim of the season, the day
before he takes his place
in the downstate office waiting
for his return, the long year
ahead, only a small framed picture
on a desk: this place
he is trying not to leave.

Something low to the water comes fast,
gliding, making its way toward the rock,
dipping, leading the wind, arriving
overhead too soon, stalling
the right wing to turn abruptly,
tilting into the sun, circling the boulder
and its naked swimmer: little more
than bones spattered with meat,
bland and bunched, trying
to become part rock, part air.

It seems to stop, casting
a huge ragged cross in shadow, its
body stretched, wings straining
their six-foot span against the glare
mostly gone except at the webbing of wings,
the connecting flesh, the membrane
where the tertial feathers become
scapular, and the swimmer

Sees through it, the translucent window
of tissue, fascia wrinkled yet clear, light
streaming through ligaments and veins, an arm's
reach away, the hoarse guttural squawk
leaving the mandibles, loose plumage emblazoned
with feathers long and ruffled, bald legs
set rigid as a clean-plucked tail, unblinking
eyes, caught in passing, a blur
of underbelly, the crook of neck tucked
for flight, a single flex of wings
lifting the Great Blue atop the wind,

Tipping the swimmer over the side, drawing
him toward the shadow skimming off

to the shallows, sending him deep, his arms
folded to his thighs like wings,
legs rigid, feet fluttering him on
through the reeds, hands coming forward
to pull him into the dark corridor
he is making, his chest closing
like a bag of air caught in a fist;
time left to rise into sunlight,
but the need slacking off as his face
feels the slim stalks reaching
for the surface long unbroken, almost still.

BLOODLINE

Her son's back is leather; wet,
it becomes her father's
russet brown, tanned by field weather
however it happened to turn;
it is the Seneca skin he kept hidden in cloth,
like something passed on in shame.

For half her life, she has failed
to bring him back through her son; and again
she kneels at the hill of stones, watching
the boy in the pond below:

He is unaware of the workshirt she sees
come up from the grave
to fit itself to his shoulders,
giving itself to water, as his arms pump
against stalks, cutting a path
toward the opposite shore, long muscles,
almost a man's, pacing themselves,
as the back goes bare, glistening with labor.

He comes up from water, trailing
a branch half his height, and slashes

the weeds as though they were there
waiting to be harvested; her lips move,
unseen, and he is gone,
into the thicket, her hand near, stretched
across the pond, selecting a tree
for its strength.

He climbs a clearing limb, and walks
until it bends, filling his lungs
with sunlight, his shadow
laid like cloth on the pond; he folds
himself in half, and enters without sound,
surfacing a long way from shore,
his gaunt face turning for air,
its features more like her father's
than before.

He will come with grain dripping off him
like water, words tumbling out, a plea
to go with him to see the world he's found;
and she will go,
always she will go, to follow his hands
and something akin to that other voice
giving names to things growing at his feet:

The adder's-tongue and bloodroot, trailing
arbutus, and ahead, bunch berries looking
like fallen dogwoods, lady slippers
near pulpits, Indian pipes white
against the peat moss floor
of an earlier spring
when her father found arrowheads and clover
in the open fields of her hidden life.

White-tail

He doesn't expect anyone hushed,
high in the leaves, waiting
on the padded shelf of a tree-stand
held fast to the softwood trunk
by straps and clamp-chains mailed
from catalogs whose pages crowd man's sleep.

He doesn't know they have given up
the 3-legged stools they used to squat on,
in a scramble of brush, a 30-aught-6
laid out and oiled across woolen thighs.

He doesn't sense the telescopic lens
selecting a point of entry on his side,
the slug moments away, as he chews the first
of a dozen low-hanging limbs encircling
the scrape: the mating ground he intends
to last the season, rut scent leaking
from the glands along his face
as he rubs them hard against the pale wound
of bark already healing from within.

The thud breaks him in half,
the impact full enough

to knock his antlers off at the crown,
to send them into air
already spattered with quiet strands
of lung blown fresh from a hole
a fist could fill, tissue settling
on the forest floor
where he feels his lost breath
sucking backward toward its source.

He cannot see the branch
they are wrenching from the tree
he is sprawled against, or feel it
going in across his open mouth, a ritual
they use, a cleansing they believe; long
as a man's bent arm: spruce—the taste
he avoided even in the darkest winters
he'd survived along the ridge of Stony Kill.

FRESH-KILL REPORT

(Predator Count, NYS Conservation Department, Form 627)

ANIMAL: Bobcat, felis rufus
GENDER: Male
AGE APPROXIMATE: Seven
WEIGHT: 20 pounds
HEIGHT: 22 inches at shoulder
TAIL: 6-inch stub, intact
TEETH: Pristine gloss
CLAWS: Hooked, unbroken
COAT: Standard, tan/grey
KILL TIME: Dusk
PURPOSE: Fur trade
PELT VALUE: $300
METHOD: .22 Magnum, solid c.l.
HIT ZONE: Right temple
COUNTY: Hamilton
LOCALE: Arbutus Pond, upper ridge

REQUIRED NARRATIVE:

Animal was put down moments after he stalked and killed sleeping deer. Observed strike: bobcat took a long measured arc and landed high on prey's back, digging in with all fours. Then, he listed to the left while deep-setting teeth in deer's throat. The strangulation was swift.

NAME OF HUNTER: _____

TODAY'S DATE: _____

SIGNATURE: _____

ADDRESS: _____

_____

LICENSE #: _____

EXPIRATION DATE: _____

REDTAIL

Jeffers knew you best.
There should be a way for you to sense
the kinship he felt, the longing
to be part of you, willing his flesh
to you, chunk by chunk: carrion baggage
fueling your flight, canceling your need to search
meals out while he lasts.

There is a thing that sets you apart
from other birds, hawk; you know it,
and your patterns show you do what you do
because you know who you are.

The small wings that chase you across clouds,
trying to peck you away from nests,
feel the whip of your wings, the clawing
of talons, the beak set for them.

You take to the cliffs of Carmel,
the tower Tor, as if in homage
to the man who brought you close
to us, lifting his spirit skyward
every time you take to air, hurling yourself
up against whatever there is there,
whatever the vast territory has to offer.

Purple Finch

They are frantic for their morning meal,
this pair: her plain brown shimmering dark
against the clapboards, his muted cowl
a blur absorbing slants of light
as they crack sunflower hulls, flicking
them left and right, leaving the kernels
balanced in place to swallow.

And now they are off for a spell
on wings shaped to fit the slipstream
of the sky, feathers trimmed by growth
to grip the air that courses through
their chambered lungs at fever pitch, bloating
the flight sacs, filling their hollow bones
to full measure until the finches
are as much air as the air
suddenly cleansed by its passage,
becoming something new, something
unlike anything
it has ever been before.

THE LIST

When he feels the night closing in,
like a jacket a size too small, tilting
the ground, skewing the clouds outside
his condo window, he squeezes his eyes
shut and plans chores, memorizing each detail
like a spy with a scribbled note to swallow.

He pictures the mountain cabin
they could have saved from demolition and puts
everything in his head on slow motion, moving
his fingers beneath the pillow
that won't bring sleep.

He could have driven there at first light
and begun: tarpaper, pungent and thick, spread
out for tacking on the rough-hewn floor;
each flathead tapped five times now
with his right forefinger, the sound coming up
through the pillow, every nail adding
to the straight silver shine extending row
after row across the 30-foot length,
the 12-foot width. Up

He finds himself up, rising up
to the ceiling and beyond, seven rolls
of tarpaper light as bedding in his arms,
enough nails sprouting from his teeth
to ward off a nightmare of porcupine.

He steadies both feet against the footboard
and hears himself hammering overhead, dust
filtering down on the covers, the pitched wood
settling under the first layer of dark,
overlapping seams, buckets of hot tar, hauled
from the fire he scratched in the bottom sheet,
hauled to the roof to be spread smooth
as bedclothes would be without him, but he stays

Put, one leg wanting to curl away. He remains
stiff-legged, knowing how to lie safe on a roof.
A hanging drop lands him on hands and knees,
leaves and small sticks sticking to palms and arms
and dungarees; he looks like a scarecrow blown in
from the fields for lunch or a nap or a book
of matches, or maybe to help in rolling out
the bottom run of tarpaper for the front wall.
The back, the sides, the front; he's done.

The cabin is wrapped, and he lays his hands
flat under the pillow, the fingers moving on their own,
unaware he is taking a break before going on
to the carpet. The knuckles are twitching
for sleep or action, but they have no choice
if the night is to be kept at bay.

It is indoor-outdoor rubber-backed weave
in the pattern he etched on his palm. It fits the room
like a liner fits its drawer. The staple-gun bangs
in his ear but the pillow dulls the shots, pinning
the carpet edge to the floor; his sleeping wife
stirs, only a slight break in her breathing.
He feels her close and goes on. Before he knows it,

The clapboards are stacked within reach,
the handsaw moving in his fist, bumping
the headboard, each cut precise, 7-hundred running
feet ready to fall into place. He balances
the first over his head, high
against the overhang, and whacks the protruding nails
home, walking first to the left, then
back to the right, pushing up and slamming in,

board butted to board, all sides of the box
he could have saved and restored.

Inside, with bricks scoring his hands, he sets
and cements a 4-by-4 base and dances
the potbelly stove into place, leaving it
firm on its four sculpted feet. Sheetrock goes up
with the flick of a wrist, the hard-asbestos
the same; chunks and chips from sawing ignite
like a scarecrow's bookmatch and send rich wet
smoke against the sky where clouds adjust the first
slant of light enough to speckle the wall by his bed.

LOON

We lie awake in dark
so black we swear
we've gone blind waiting
for your screech,
but no sound comes
until sleep takes us
long enough to be thrown
awake by the split-level
scream of the mad old lady
in your throat, lowered
there at birth, kept
for the nightly ritual
you tend to,
proclaiming this pond
as your own.

BAT

Badly maligned, nearly
  impossible to track until the search
    is done, and then you appear
as if summoned, swooping from the settling dusk
    or flexing what should be cardboard
  wings on that shriveled mouse
    body when we lift a slab
of wood from under the cabin porch, peat
    moss soft beneath your belly,
the hiss spitting out from triangled lips or beak
  or whatever it is that leaves a check mark
    on a girl's cheekbone: a scold to stay out
of deserted houses, to let your kind be, no brooms
    no sticks no shoes or baseball caps,
      nothing but the edge
    of this shovel held hard
      against your neck, stopping
    the night air from being sucked in,
  puffed out, all this earth
  surrounding you scraped up aside
  the hole we bury you in,
    that tainted soil, rabid
even if not, pushed in on your dried leather,

cleaner dirt, then a flat stone,
          heavier than it needs to be, weighing you
     down where you belong, the sound
of your warning set deep under our skulls, able
   to wake us at whim, the sky ready to drop
        kin who can tangle themselves in our hair,
screech our ears off at the roots, nothing
   we learn changing our faith in your malevolent ways,
        our only blessing large in knowing
            we are not in regions close
        as northern Mexico where you would crave
blood meals, your folded ears and tiny
   leaf-like nose close to a feeding-site, more often
than not a barefoot sleeping man, his neck
safe due to your fondness for feet, now
        where you hunch to scrape a feasting-wound,
   holding on lightly, unnoticed, your dark tongue
            lapping at the pad of a big toe.

Duff's Tavern

It's simple enough: pay
when you're served
and don't look anybody in the eye.
That way, you cut your chances
of annoying anyone and save yourself
a trip out back for a whuppin.

There are bowls of bar-nuts, but
not for you. And the hardboiled eggs
are for the regulars.

The three stools at the far end
are for Duff's sons. You
don't want to meet them. The door
marked Office has a urinal and sink,
but that's kind of private like.

Just have your beer, don't come on
friendly, and whatever you do, don't
leave a tip. Duff doesn't like that.
He'd take you out back for less.

LOCKED IN THE ICEHOUSE

Nasty as an old cigar butt, he'd sit
on the loading dock, his nub-legged chair
at a tilt to the door, heels hooked
in the top rung, thirty ton of ice safe
in canvas tarps on the huge plank shelves
he'd built by himself two wars ago.

You could see his tongs on the nearest nail,
hung open, about to swallow
the leather sheath and pear-handled ice pick
stuck within reach of his chopping hand.
The rubber apron, caught on a grappling hook,
sagged upside down on its belt.

The platform was edged in sheet metal;
truck tubes, folded and cut,
covered the corners. He'd squint at the sun
burning through his torn-umbrella canopy
and wait for cars to turn down the alley, ready
to curse them if they did and damn them
if they didn't. Mostly they didn't.

Nobody missed him,
until some neighbor's icebox went dry,

way too late to save him from the last things
he ever saw. There's that Jamison Lock
& Plunger plate on the door: brass, bigger
than a belt buckle, eight screws
holding her on. Must have been his heart.
No windows to break out, tin walls,
below freezing by a degree or two, and him
in a tee-shirt and dungarees.

But you have to be in there, afraid
to come out for an hour or two, if you're going
to know what it's really like. Like when
you're nine years old and barefoot
and stealing ice shavings, and he comes in
but doesn't see you, maybe, and goes back out
and sits in his chair forever. That's cold.
Chain hoists and hooks
dangling from the ceiling, your breath
going white as cigarette smoke.

You had to wait
until he came in for a fifty-pounder,
way in the back with that pad of burlap
over his shoulder. Then you ran for it.

The floor's all wet with splinters,
but he had boots. You could see them
when they carried him out. Dead as a doornail
was the way one yardman put it. Hard as a rock
was another. But colder than a mackerel
seemed best, considering.

DEEP

Town kid
sitting
on a
neighbor's
dock
eyeing
a frog
with a
fist-sized
rock.
Frog
garumphs
and
the kid
lets
rip;
misses
by a
mile
but
starts
to slip.
Town kid

drowning
near a
neighbor's
dock.
Frog
garumphs
at the
sinking
rock.

Warning to Tourists

*(whose kids like to light-finger
country stores)*

If you are with them, keep them
in tow. Leash 'em, collar 'em, hobble 'em;
there's bakery string and boat rope,
baling wire and clothesline (aisle three).
The shelves are loaded and the sightlines
are clear. It's as though Macy's, Bean,
and Toys 'Я' Us stashed their inventory here,
and Hoss is watching.

Why, a few summers back, a whole brigade
of "On my honor I will do my best to rip you
off" scouts arrived—let loose at Hoss's
while their keepers sucked cokes outside.
Fingers were dancing at every counter,
little city slickers come to bumpkinville,
magic about to begin: now you see it,
now you don't.

Hoss's voice took to the rafters,
from the prime beef to the coffee mugs,
up the stairs to boots and slickers
and back down to the periodicals
and candy bars, all in current danger

of being spirited away inside tee-shirts
and camping shorts fresh from home.
"Anyone within the range of my voice
who is less than sixteen years of age
will put his hands in his pockets
and leave them there and begin whistling
and will continue to do so until he arrives
at the front exit. Let's hear it!"

And the music was lovely. A boy,
whose nose ran ahead of him,
gave a nervous rendition of "God Bless
America" that played well with a hurried
go at "Mary Had A Little Lamb." "Amazing
Grace" became part of Rudolph's nose,
and a frightened scholar drawn from
the book section pursed his way through
something akin to Mozart's "Andante
in C Major for Flute and Piano."

And the store was safe and the crowd
diminished and the socks and belts
and wooden nickels and cheese and crackers

and stickers and jackknives were in place,
and the compasses all pointed north
where Hoss was watching.

Aunt Sadie's Carrot Juice

was terrible. Lukewarm and laced with dill,
it lay like swamp water
in tumblers too big for the tray she held
waist high at the cabin gate.

We'd take it down in a single gulp
and make believe it made our day,
and get another morning free
at her pitiful stretch of pond.

She'd sit on the porch out back
and shred a bunch or two, plopping the pulp
into a homemade smasher she kept tied
to the railing with string.

She never drank the stuff herself,
but the neighbor lady did: bald to the back
of her scalp she'd come, empty mug in hand,
the whiskers under her chin curled
every which way from yesterday's sleep
in the sunken chair we'd see her in
when we'd make our house-to-house rounds
through the brush-path after dark.

And Sadie wrote stacks of poems. Worse
than carrot juice, they yellowed and staled
in the summer heat, weighing down the straw
mattress in the extra room.

The thirsty neighbor found her there
in '45, sprawled dead on her poems, the piles
spilled and scattered, the last crate
of carrots going bad in the shed.

Note to Summer Renters

When the Coleman lantern starts to go,
starts to tip off the deck railing, where
it shouldn't have been to start with,
you can always lay your palm on the hollow
top-nut that holds the shade in place.

But not after the lantern's been blazing
for more than ten seconds or so. Now,
you have a hellish welt and yelling
won't make it go away. Take a good look;
take in the shape: a wintergreen lifesaver
burn melted in place for a week, maybe two.

Fill the fish bucket with lake water
and add as much ice as you have on hand,
so to speak, and keep your open fist dunked
in there till the doctor happens by.

He's in town most Fridays.

COULTER'S ROAD

Alone on his daughter's verandah,
the mountains he used to work behind him,
he'd fold the front page of the paper
in half and half again, fashioning a hat
in nothing flat.

There was a Napoleon, the bishop,
a fireman and dunce, and even one
he called Old Man Delaney's Hat.

Each rim held a headline
and he wore it for the day.

When he died, some neighbor kids waited
for the obit page and tried
to make a hat, tried to have his name
along the crown, but it always came out
sideways, no matter the pattern,
no matter the fold.

MINK

Dead, ensnared
by a 6-pack carryall: one
aluminum can still dangling.
Decomposed body, red-brown fur,
foot-and-a-half long, half-foot
tail, pale chin, underbelly
spotted white. Plastic lichen
everywhere: chip sacks, margarine
tubs, filter tips, coffee cups,
double-liter cokers, bare bottles
busted up and waiting like glowstones
to slice a paw or tongue. Slick wraps
of allsorts, brand names loosening
their colors every rain to run blood
red and bile green into the filling pond.

BEAVER

Bad eyes, good ears and snout, I know
you're there, quiet as death on the sleeping shelf
you fashioned beneath my hobnail boots;
I'm in them and squatting atop this barricade,
this sprawling island, this hodgepodge lodge
of branches and mud, saplings and logs
interlaced low at the shallow floor of the pond,
the air chute cluttered in its crisscross sticks,
steaming your fetid smell into the biting air.

Rodent, biggest of them all, roamer
amongst sedges where bur reed and lilies
blend with cattails and duckweed,
coarse grass, most anything will do to
patchwork the dam that keeps your doorways sunken,
their poke-sticks rimming the thresholds.

No bear, no bobcat, wolf or lynx would take you
on in water, but your newborn kits, webbed paws
still fragile, are nothing more than snacks
for otter and mink, an easy mark
for snapping turtles and 3-foot pike, the unseen
hawks overhead, ready to drop to rise well burdened.

Stay where you are, lake-slapper; spread some
gland grease on and go at it with your grooming
claws; end the day safe on the shelf, back leg up,
picking your teeth clean of splinters; dry out
the coat some hunter dreams of stitching
round his head, waterproof as rubber,
warm as double wool.

Varying Hare

Your good luck foot, hacked and healed
for a keyring, hangs loose on a cuphook
at our pantry door; still smooth as down,
its mild claws are poised to scratch an ear
into ecstasy with such precision
that a moment would satisfy the need.

Elsewhere, they dangle from beltclips, jalopy
mirrors, handlebars, and lie lost
in dresser drawers and bottoms of castoff
handbags, each paw soft enough to stroke,
to brush against a cheek, to fluff-up
and smooth-out, every one once
part of a matched set.

Your kind has never learned, never will;
the woodsmen know your fur, marbled,
as you scurry full tilt across leaves strewn
with first snow; when you go white,
their number swells, blood pounding, mouths
drying for the chase, hip flasks at the ready.

It is your insistence on staying
above ground that gives them the edge;

you will run their hounds forever, hours
at a time, through ditch banks and brush-grown
fencerows, mountain thickets, evergreen
swamps and alder, disappearing in willow tangles
only to emerge torn and spent, leaking blood,
stubborn in the windfalls, your scent drifting
to the snouts of exhausted dogs, triggering
their belling bark, pulling their masters
through the night woods to your stained thawing bier.

A single round, point blank, will do,
a blade drawn glinting beneath your infant squeal,
feet clipped off and kept, your pelt scraped
clean; most of what you were flung
onto the crotch of a tree, light snow disturbed,
accepting the only color you have left to give.

SUDDEN ENCOUNTER

If there's no shoulder hump,
it's no grizzly; you've found yourself
a black bear, no matter what shade
of glossy shag she's wearing this season.

If she goes for you: swatting the ground,
snorting, blowing, roaring, moaning,
just back off. Don't play dead. Don't
climb a tree. Don't run for it.

If she hasn't charged but is there taking
a long look, you'd better throw a fit: flail
your arms, twist and shout, bang some pans, do a
dance, swat your heels, whistle, scream, honk and hoot.
Still there? Then bark
and shriek, sneeze, cough, gargle and gurgle, huff
and puff, snarl and roar, growl and bawl and bellow.
If she's gone, backtrack and head
for home, cracking the air
with all the racket you can muster.

But, if she charges and keeps on coming,
and you forgot to bring your .458 Magnum

and 510-gr. soft-point bullets, and you
neglected to pack that handheld airhorn
from your 18-wheeler, and the capsaicin repellent
spray is back home sitting on the windowsill
like a teddybear, you'd better find a hardside shelter fast
or settle in for an open-air bar fight. Get
something: pots to clang in her ear, an axe or stout branch
for snout-bashing, a rock, a buckknife; and let loose
some noises. At least her teeth have no
shearing blades like the neighbor's cat. Small

Comfort? Well, that's so. But give it to her
good. Smack her up side the head. Get right up
in her face and give her what for, break some teeth,
kick some butt, gouge an eyeball or two.
You might get lucky; she could up
and turn away, wander off. If not,
you'll never know the difference.

VERBATIM

Well, you've got your silky pocket mouse,
the pale kangaroo mouse, the wood
mouse, the classic mosaic-tail mouse,
the hopping mouse and the northern birch
mouse. But this,
this is your basic house mouse.

Flat as a nickel pancake he came
under the cabin door, avoiding walls
secured with steel wool, window screening,
and 45 yards of hardware cloth. Finicky,
compulsive, nearsighted, in search of cheese,
soap, glue, goobers, chocolate and tootsie
rolls, he settled for plain old peanut butter
painstakingly tangled in a foot
of cotton-covered polyester button thread
snag-tied to the lip of a snap-trap's pallet.

Now, good as dead, his legs in disarray,
the tiny teeth smeared with bait,
his unclosed eyes still give off a dying light
despite the spring-sprung bar, neck high
that took his breath away.

His kind have kept the trait
their long-gone kin brought in from overseas
in 1543: an excretion rate of 50
droppings every day,
300 spurts of urine in between. We salute
them now in quick remorse and bury him
at sea, remembering to flush. Vowing
better barricades, we do not set the trap,
but try for sleep, sensing guilt
may only bring us dreams of mountain
quilts filling up with furry things.

SNACK

When the cabin lights go out,
they begin to arrive, fashionably late,
from the trees overhanging the pond.

Backing their way down the thick crust
of the hemlock, each stiletto of their paws,
they know, will hold them fast till they let go.

Here they come, landing as agile as gymnasts,
their gunman's masks intact, in fact ingrown, their
raccoon coats buttonless, for now.

Single file, up the porch steps they stroll,
guests, a party of six, all business already, bent
to the task of sampling the spattered grease
along our stained plank floor. One up, two up
to the barbecue that moves sideways on its wheels;
no fear, they know such things, even to scrape

And lick and wipe and pick at both sides
of the grills until they shine above the coals
they leave alone to turn to dust.

Three are before us on the table we keep
pressed against the wall. They've come to see
what they can see inside and what they see
is us, our noses tight against the windowpane
to see what we can see of them, and see
their steak-smeared mugs full-face, tongues

Wagging like napkins cleaning up the mess,
their grungy paws held half limp as though we
are the ones to bring them supping-rags dunked
in water warmed with lime and sided by tea-towels
and a dainty tray of mints. No deal and so

They leave to rise again to quarters closer
to the sky, our flashlights giving cloudy chase,
but clear enough to see them turn, as they deign to do,
partway in their trek, to see us standing barefoot
dressed in stripes and dots up to our craning necks.

GETTING READY FOR SNOW

The cellar trunk opens to dust,
its mothball breath unfolding with wools
set there last spring when we felt
we might be sharing the last
of our seasons together;
but now, a bonus of days.

The hooded jackets, their gloves
supple enough to eat; deep in one pocket,
a kleenex, grey and untouchable
as a dead mouse found in the rafters.

Then come the leggings harsh as wicker,
and boots ready for the back fields
where toboggans run all winter,
and a forgotten helmet
fitting no one this year.

Clothing done, we turn to outer things:
gutters banked with leaves, the shed
waiting to be stacked with wood;

Nothing so suits such a day
as the raised arm falling, making its mark

on the crack of any log, scattering slabs
enough to warm the bones through
the given nights ahead.

AFTER THREE DAYS ALONE

There are trees enough
       for both her eyes
And sky enough
       to overflow this place;
Afloat, we'd arch as one
       and go so deep
I'd lose her there
       as though in sleep,
Before we'd rise
       to find the sun
Within her hair
       across her face.

Inside the shack
       there is no light,
Just lanterns all in need of fuel;
       the canvas sack
Has lost its ice, all
       food untouched and barely cool;
The bed against the darkest wall
       will go unused again tonight.

CABIN FEVER

Her breathing's all stuttery, eyes tight
On the wall—all log, well-packed, 3-inch

Insulation beyond, tongue-and-groove
Clapboarding out front taking the storm.

Her Great Aunt Velma's quilt high-tacked
With Pancher nails, hanging kitty-corner

To the bed, but the wind whistles through.
Flannel nightgown, knotweave sweaters buttoned

Up, long johns, pajama bottoms tucked inside
Heavy wool boot-socks, a shawl

Wound well around her neck and head, still
She can't get warm, shivering not ten feet

From the potbelly jammed with wood she cut
And stacked last spring; that old boiling-kettle

Spitting out steam for the lungs. Winter sheets,
Three army blankets, a store-bought thermal

Spread beneath them. Extra blankets,
Rolled tight as sausage, piled all along

The sidewall and turned to run the headboard,
Three high. Better than a hundred degrees.

Snow's been coming since early afternoon
And won't be stopping anytime soon

From the looks of it; the windows are full,
The door heaving against its bolt, wires down,

Road's gone. Must be plenty left to do,
But for the life of her, she can't bring it to mind.

KACHUNK

Tik-a-tah, tik-a-tah
   ka-ting, ka-ting
     ka-tah, ka-tah
   ting-ting, ka-ting, ka-ting
Ka-tah, ka-tah, kachunk

Chainsaw coolin from a morning run
Whittled sticks drummin on a clean-cut stump
Wet as a snarehead spilled with beer

Right foot thumpin on the forest floor:
White-orange sawdust as it used to be
On the black wood planks of The Kitty Kat Klub

Delaware bus to the end of the line
Drumsticks tickin on his bony knees
Kah-tah, ka-ting

Walk the side streets away from town
Friday night in Buffalo, turn at Genesee
Keep sticks workin all the way:

Trash can, car top, hood and grille
Ka-tah, ka-tah, ting-chunk

Tic-a-tic-a-tic-a-tic, ka-tah
Side door open, slide on in,
Sit in the shadows, not a word
Too young for drinks, count the drunks

Sticks still flickin between his legs
Tik-a-tah, tik-a-tah, kachunk, kachunk
Spider Thompson walkin the bar
Spider Thompson doin The Bird
Drumsticks tappin on a barroom chair
Drumsticks tappin on a clean-cut stump
Kachunk

CONNEMARA

In a field of stones,
the house is stone,
a chimney scant with twisted smoke,
its roof's worn thatch long since assigned
to vagrant crows in search of things
that crawl or fly at dawn.

Inside the single room,
a man moves lightly in his chair,
lays his palms across his eyes
and mumbles something to the rain
that's started up again.

He pulls the woolen lap-robe
to his chin and tastes the smouldering peat
that swirls at him, up from the hearth
where shadows burnt the walls all night.

He wears the woolen suit and vest he wore
to market all those years. The shoes
are dried beyond repair. The necktie
he'll be waked in dangles from a low beam
overhead, its four-in-hand knot in place.

He knows no need to leave or stay,
but there's a spoon or two of tea left
in the jar somewhere behind him on a shelf,
he's sure, and a crust of bread, he thinks,
as well. There'll be no going out
this day.

RUDY

Whenever he's alone too long,
he does it: cups his hands and looks
inside, adjusting the amount of light
by moving his fingers, closing it off
when he sees too much, too little, his
eyelashes flicking against his thumbs,
the left eye clamped shut, elbows on knees,
this time, settled on a rock in the woods
twelve, thirteen feet from the shack
he's made do with, its kerosene light spilling
out a window shape that includes his head
and hands; the rest set apart in the night
that is closing in around him.

He wants something in there
and snaps a twig from a berry bush
that has become almost an annoyance
at his side. He cracks the stem nearly
in half and slides it in, onto his lefthand
palm and covers it with the right,
tumbling it to the front with a quick tilt,
another. Dark, he keeps it dark, even
the sighthole closed off. "There,"
he says, "what do you think of that."

And then he gives it a scratch of light;
he sees the twig as many things, common things
at first: twig as twig, a bent nail, an arm
twig, a curled lock of a woman's hair. But then,
the other twig things arrive to spoil it,
slim rays of light giving them time, close up
as they slide through the lid
into the vitreous, into the brain, no matter
how quick he is to flick his fingers
straight out, dropping the twig onto the ground,
grinding it to smithereens with the heel
of his boot then the other boot, time
and again, trying hard to the end.

PARTICULARS

When they reach his lot,
there will be a fence; the gate
is always locked. The dogs
are large and anxious to prove
their worth as they prowl
the perimeter, sniffing the air
for a taste of unfamiliar breath.
Their bark activates floodlights
screwed to the upper limbs of oaks.
At his bedside, a holster
gathers dust around its piece,
the slightest trace of oil
making its presence known in the dark.
They should stay home.
He will kill them all in turn.

She Wanted to Know

why her brother, eighteen
months younger, not even
in his teens, could go off
through the woods alone, and she
couldn't—couldn't understand
her father, his fears of what might be
out there: Never mind what,
he said, I know what
I'm talking about; trees that look
like things aren't always trees—
and he went on splitting wood for them
to stack by dusk, but she kept after him
until he lost control and slammed his axe
into the chopping block to punctuate
the final No, and kicked the empty water bucket
toward the pond, only to watch it veer off
to the right, curving straight
for her startled face, aiming to change it
by half, and only luck let it go
clanking down the path, sending her off
to find her mother, leaving him
to face his son who hadn't come
to understand the dark-slab forest any more
than his sister had.

NOW AND AGAIN

He sits on the wooden bench nailed fast
to the cabin wall and writes it all down,
as he always does, meticulously, devoted
to detail, as though he'd observed it all
from afar, as though he were free of it,
at last, each hand doing its part, flattening
the page, steering the pencil along the blue
lines of the tablet cracked open across his knees,
letters too cramped to be read, some starting to gouge
through, others climbing the margin, scudding off
into the empty space beside him, the holding-thumb
shivering in place, the inadequate stub
flying away from his grip to skid out of sight
into the cot's long shadow: one of the many
places he knows he must never explore.

DIRECT HIT

Your beagle mutt remembers your boot,
the hunt, the burst of pleasure
in your throat as he felt the arrow
take him down at short range.

He has no mind for the lie you gave
the vet: unseen hunters drunk
and barking back before one took his aim.

If he could raise his head
from the blanket, he would try
to give the truth to the woman who sings
through her darkest chores, half aware
of shadows building behind your eyes.

But it is for him to cower, waiting out
the day before making his last escape
slow into the winter mountains he knows
must become his home.

CHOW CHOW

(Liontamer Bertha 11/6/77 – 4/28/88)

But now I lay you down to sleep, dead weight
In a grey blanket, across the same back seat
You'd take to on command and sit straight-legged,
Alert to drivers caught in double-takes of you.

Tonight, you are no more
Than a sack of leaves dry in my arms.
The wet cloth against your mouth will not
Coax your jaws apart. Only your mild
Exhausted breath tells us you are here,
Your head slack upon the lap that held you
As a pup, the soothing voice in concert
With the hand smoothing the coat it used
To groom. Your fur comes loose
In handfuls; it carries scents of sick wards,
Sour flesh unable to control itself.

The vet is waiting after hours.
The parking lot is dark. The slightest tug
Steers you toward the room of tiles, chrome,
And light. Again we lift your empty weight
And put you down. Just once you make a sound,
A yip, a breaking in the throat. We listen

To the verdict: strokes, cataracts closing
In, some dread thing growing deep inside.
To the end, you flag your tail, forward
On your back, the way it would have been in show.
We take you close and watch the plugged-in razor
Shave a patch into your paw. We feel your skullbone
Hard against our lips and say goodbye.

STARTING OVER

Took two lynx out near Grayling yesterday,
females. Three males over by Logan
and Devil's Paw. Used those padded legtraps
and rubber tethers; stopped all five cold.

Double your common housecat, long
as a yardstick slung with muscles, greytan
scattered with spots, furry ruff,
tufted ears tufted
cheeks, black-tip tail.

Had to gunnysack them down to Yukon Air,
Gustafson crates, extra rods and straps
all around, Flight #37 to Albany,
then on to Newcomb by van.

Haven't been any in those mountains
for a hundred years or more,
but they're back now, set free to roam
the high peaks of the park, safe
from bobcat and coyote, even the fisher,
that rarified air not to their liking,
leaving a bounty of snowshoe hare:

Fair game for five broad-footed cats
ready for night duty, getting used
to eartags grown clean into wounds,
mercury-tilt collars snug on their necks
sending pulsing notes back to range stations,
five fragile songs caught in midair
by those who gave them names
like Jim and Howler and Q2.

Red pushpins are starting to dot
the hacking-map, six million acres
filling the back wall, crowding the window
that lets the Adirondacks in—bare
and green, perfect cover
for their far-flung escapes, all alone,
apart till spring, when Cearse and Tanya
will choose den sites and wait
for the others to find them.

LEAVING

Now it is time,
before the weather goes sour;
we will take what we can:
a change of clothes, a few tools,
your medicines.

There will be plenty to eat:
nuts and berries, cattail roots,
grasshoppers, minnows, grubs;
you'll be all right; you'll see.

Things will seem better
when we are on the move; for now,
forget last night; remember
only that we are here, alive,
able to forage for ourselves;
that is more than we deserve.

Look at me; for my part,
I am sorry; I cannot say more.
If we are to leave, it must be now.
Come; don't make me go by myself.

Winter Sleep

He hadn't meant to wander off or lose
The path the way he did, still warm, his coat
Unbuttoned to his belt, the work boots she
Had laced for him, a pair of canvas gloves
In case he found some kindling low enough
To snap, to stash beneath his arm the way
He used to do before he lost his grasp

On things, back when his words meant what he said.
And even now he tries a test but can
Not name the town his wife is visiting;
He shakes his head from side to side and squints
His eyes until the droning hollow note
He sometimes hears for hours at a time
Goes drifting off among the forest pines

He's owned for all these married forty years
But does not recognize. He tells himself
To start a circle-walk and all comes clear.
His broken gait goes wide until he finds
A trail. He hurries on his way until
He thinks he sees the cabin held against
Some unnamed day's last light. His throat is dry,

His legs are taking chill. He kicks the trip
Root waiting there; it snares him hard and sits
Him down, just slightly dazed, upon the ground.
He finds himself beside a hemlock trunk,
Its branches sagging heavy with their snow.
A remnant of a leash hangs close above
His head; it might not be the one they tied

Their springer spaniel to each afternoon
For naps, that same old dog who loved to take
On head-to-head most anything on fours
Until he took an antler deep in fur.
The leash's nail is halved by rust, its chain
Pulls free against his chest, a talisman
He fondles well before he shuts his eyes

To speak her name out loud and see her warm
And safe there in her mother's den, with tea
And danish pastry by the fire, attuned
To one another's world gone wrong, aware
Of family time that's measured out like cloth.
The leash is cold but gives him memory:
Good dog, here dog. Come on, he'd say, and Beau

Would go to him all dripping wet from yet
Another hunting-swim, or running drool
From racing through the brush, and ready now
To lie this close, his head between his paws,
Content to have a hand that's laid to rest
Upon his back. A winter sleep comes soon,
And change of breathing too, a shudder from

His dreams, if dreams still build their broken flame
Within a leather thong that's too long dead
And empty now. He stirs and knows he should
Be up and on his way, but can't begin
To tell himself the thing he ought to do,
So settles back against the tree and wants
The cabin that he sees, no more than half

A walk away, to be his own; the door
Is darkened oak, the wooden roof's thick ice
Recast beneath a bit of smoke still caught
Adrift without its stove and moving fast
Into a breeze becoming wind, large flakes
Of snow diminishing to salt. Across
The changing crust he sees the wood he could

Have stacked that way some other place or time.
It looks like theirs: a standing hardwood cord,
All split and covered with a tarp. If he'd
Disturb the pile enough he'd have a slant
Against the snow, a place to curl up in,
And rest his eyes and hands and shut away
The night whose sounds are staying in his head

Much longer than he thinks they should. If he
Could only see the upper window like
The one she's gone to in the past to watch
Him working down below, to wave and press
Her face against the glass. If she were there,
She'd see him here. She may have tried to phone.
If so, she's on the logging road by now.

She'd never leave him in the woods this far
From home. He whimpers to himself and vows
To stay awake until she comes. He hopes
She is all right. Not good to drive alone
This time of year at night. He'll be relieved
When she gets home. Mulled cider would be good.
And cheddar cheese shaved thin on homemade bread.

She should have left a light on for his sake.
He cannot see a window anywhere,
But thinks of how they'll stand there looking out,
The snow quite soft and quick in coming in.
The leash is gone and both his gloves, his hands
Are open at arm's length, allowing snow
To land upon his palms. He'll close them tight

When they are full; the snow's good packing, wet
Enough to throw. The night is very loud,
But he is taken by the woods, his hands,
The storm, the thought of all these trees they chose
To be with all these years. He looks into
The ground and then against the crowded air
And tastes the dark accumulation there.